Stepmotherland

"In *Stepmotherland*, Darrel Alejand
lines to script-like dialogue to gorg
search for a language that can properly articulate what home is. . . .
This book is a kind of coming of age into brilliance."
—Jericho Brown, author of *The Tradition*,
winner of the Pulitzer Prize

"*Stepmotherland* is the brilliant and vertiginous movement of a soul
from the state of innocence to experience and a remarkable and
groundbreaking collection. No one who reads these stunning
poems is likely to remain unmoved or unchanged by them."
—Lorna Goodison, author of *Supplying Salt and Light*
and former Poet Laureate of Jamaica

"*Stepmotherland* is a balm. The lyrics to a melody that has always
played in our heads. Holnes gives us the heartbreaking and
healing song. A stunning debut."
—Jacqueline Woodson, author of *Brown Girl Dreaming*
and winner of the National Book Award

"Darrel Alejandro Holnes navigates the fraught politics of national,
racial, and sexual identities with grace and wisdom beyond his years
in order to locate that precarious but remarkable space that a queer
Afro/Black-Latino immigrant from Panamá can call home. . . .
What a unique, multivalent, and incredibly moving debut."
—Rigoberto González, author of *The Book of Ruin*
and winner of the Lambda Literary Award

STEPMOTHERLAND

THE ANDRÉS MONTOYA POETRY PRIZE

2004, *Pity the Drowned Horses*, Sheryl Luna
Final Judge: Robert Vazquez

2006, *The Outer Bands*, Gabriel Gomez
Final Judge: Valerie Martínez

2008, *My Kill Adore Him*, Paul Martínez Pompa
Final Judge: Martín Espada

2010, *Tropicalia*, Emma Trelles
Final Judge: Silvia Curbelo

2012, *A Tongue in the Mouth of the Dying*, Laurie Anne Guerrero
Final Judge: Francisco X. Alarcón

2014, *Furious Dusk*, David Campos
Final Judge: Rhina P. Espaillat

2016, *Of Form & Gather*, Felicia Zamora
Final Judge: Edwin Torres

2018, *The Inheritance of Haunting*, Heidi Andrea Restrepo Rhodes
Final Judge: Ada Limón

2022, *Stepmotherland*, Darrel Alejandro Holnes
Final Judge: John Murillo

The Andrés Montoya Poetry Prize, named after the late California native and author of the award-winning book, *The Iceworker Sings and Other Poems*, and the posthumous volume, *A Jury of Trees*, supports the publication of a first book by a Latinx poet. Awarded every other year, the prize is administered by Letras Latinas—the literary initiative at the University of Notre Dame's Institute for Latino Studies.

STEPMOTHERLAND

Darrel Alejandro Holnes

University of Notre Dame Press
Notre Dame, Indiana

University of Notre Dame Press
Notre Dame, Indiana 46556
undpress.nd.edu

Title page art: "Abya Yala, Dame Tú Mano" by Patricia Encarnación. Used with permission

Published in the United States of America

Library of Congress Control Number: 2021948793

ISBN: 978-0-268-20215-6 (Hardback)
ISBN: 978-0-268-20216-3 (Paperback)
ISBN: 978-0-268-20217-0 (WebPDF)
ISBN: 978-0-268-20214-9 (Epub)

for my mothers

para mis madres

Contents

CITIZEN

PATRIOT

Acknowledgments

Grateful acknowledgment is made to the editors of the following publications in which these poems, or earlier versions of them, have appeared: Academy of American Poets' Poem-A-Day, *Assaracus, American Poetry Review, The Caribbean Writer, Common Knowledge, Day One* (Amazon), *decomP* magazine, *Foglifter Journal, Glass: A Journal of Poetry, Grand Literary Journal, Gulf Coast: A Journal of Literature and Fine Arts, HEArt Online: Human Equity Through Art, Kweli, Lambda Literary, Mason's Road, Mead: The Magazine of Literature and Libations, NACLA* (North American Congress on Latin America), *Nimrod International Journal, Oberon Poetry Magazine, Poetry International, Split This Rock, The Feminist Wire, The Portable Boog Reader, The Puritan, Wilde Magazine,* and *Wordpeace.*

I am also grateful to the editors of the following anthologies and books, where some of these poems have appeared: *Best American Experimental Writing, Between: New Gay Poetry, Furious Flower: Seeding the Future of African American Poetry, Multilingual Anthology: The Americas Poetry Festival of New York, PRIME: Poetry & Conversation, The Queer South: LGBTQ Writers on the American South, Two Countries: U.S. Daughters & Sons of Immigrant Parents,* and *The Wandering Song: Central American Writing in the United States.*

Thanks to John Murillo, the Andrés Montoya family, Letras Latinas, and to my entire team at Notre Dame University Press. Special thanks to family, friends, teachers, and colleagues who have supported my writing throughout the years: my family, Jacinto Holnes, Nelida Gournet de Holnes, and Krystle Holnes, and colleagues and editors, Opal Palmer Adison, Rosebud Ben-Oni, Bryan Borland, Carl Ciaramitaro, Tafisha Edwards, Hafizah Geter, William Johnson, David Tomas Martinez, Jerome Ellison Murphy, Fred Sasaki, Elizabeth Scanlon, Stewart Shaw, Elizabeth Senja Spackman, L. Lamar Wilson, J. Preston Witt, and Javier Zamora. Special thanks to tía Ivonne Machado.

Additional thanks to the Bread Loaf Writers' Conference, Cave Canem, Canto Mundo, MacDowell, Marble House Project, Rose O'Neill Literary

House, the Vermont College of Fine Arts, the University of Michigan – Ann Arbor's Helen Zell Writers' Program, and the University of Houston faculty and literary communities.

Major thanks to the National Endowment of the Arts and the Jerome Foundation for their support.

These Poems Stand on Indigenous Land

The poems in this collection are dedicated to my ancestors, those who were brought to the Americas, and those who were already there. As a person of African descent who is also of Chocó descent, it's important for me to acknowledge the history of the lands on which I stood to write these poems.

Many of the cities in which I've resided and institutions I have attended exist because of the removal of Indigenous people, a removal and erasure from which these institutions and communities continue to benefit. I acknowledge that history and offer this acknowledgment to pay respect to all Indigenous ancestors and stand against their erasure and to offer my gratitude for their guidance when writing these poems.

In crafting this statement, a best-effort approach was used. It by no means is complete or perfect as information on land and information on sacred connection is not readily accessible due to violent colonization and resulting community fragmentation. This statement does not represent or intend to represent official or legal affiliations of any Indigenous nations, nor do I represent any nations with this statement. For more information, please contact the nations directly.

I am thankful to consultant Madeline Easley of the Wyandotte Nation of Oklahoma for helping me craft this page and the land acknowledgment statement on the following page.

—Darrel Alejandro Holnes

Land Acknowledgment Statement

This statement is to acknowledge that the poems in this book were written while the poet took private residence, was a poet-in-residence, or was a student at institutions, on Indigenous land of the following groups:

- Panama: Ngäbe (Guaymí*), Buglé (Bokota), Guna (Kuna), Chocó (Emberá and Wounaan), Bribri, and Naso Tjër Di (Teribe)
- United States of America:
  - Manhattan, NY: Munsee Lenape and Wappinger
  - Houston, TX: Karankawa, Coahuiltecan, Atakapa-Ishak, and Sana
  - Crown Heights, Brooklyn, NY: Munsee Lenape and Canarsie
  - Bread Loaf Writers Conference at Middlebury College, Middlebury, VT: Mohican, Wabanaki, and Abenaki
  - Vermont College of Fine Arts, Montpelier, VT: Wabanaki and Abenaki
  - Marble House, Dorset, VT: Mohican, Wabanaki, and Abenaki
  - MacDowell, Peterborough, NH: Pennacook, Wabanaki, and Abenaki
  - Cave Canem Summer Retreat, Greensburg, PA: Osage
  - Rose O'Neill Literary House, Chestertown, MD: Susquehannock, Nentego (Nanticoke), and Piscataway
  - University of Michigan—Ann Arbor, MI: Meškwahki·aša·hina (Fox), Peoria, Anishinabewaki, and Bodéwadmiakiwen
    * Guaymí is a recently outdated term to refer to the Ngäbe people.

Source: Native Land Digital

"Despite centuries of colonial theft and violence, this is still Indigenous land. It will always be Indigenous land."

—Native Governance Center

Introduction to the Poems

Darrel Alejandro Holnes is a poet of promise and vision. And *Stepmotherland* is a promising and visionary debut. In this vital first collection, Holnes displays an impressive range of both subject and sensibility. Whether working in more traditional lyric, narrative, and lyric-narrative modes, or experimenting with nonce forms derived from theater, geometry, and even dictionary entry formats, Holnes's poems exhibit a lively imagination and keen intellect. At turns erotic, often political, and always vulnerable, *Stepmotherland* provides the reader a fresh perspective on the countless ways in which history—personal, national—can, by its very nature, blur the lines between witness and participant, between *doer* and *done to.*

The best of Holnes's work moves in, but is not encumbered by, what we have come to know as the tradition of *witness.* Characterized by some of its practitioners as a mode of writing that combines the personal and political, poetry of witness often takes as its subject the lived experience of those most directly affected by the world's chronic power imbalances and the practices carried out in order to maintain them. Poems often depict firsthand accounts of war, political imprisonment, torture, forced exile, and so on. Here, Holnes has us covered. In the book's first section, specifically in such poems as "Scenes from Operation Just Cause," "20 de Diciembre, 1989: When the U.S. Invades Panamá," and "When the Narcos Kidnap JuanFe," he grounds us in the reality (and surreality) of a people trying to make a way while caught in the crossfire of world powers, corrupt dictators, and drug cartels. Should he have played this one note throughout the rest of the collection, Holnes may have given us a compelling enough song and would have satisfied the conventional expectations of witness, but he would not have satisfied his own incisive nature. Holnes understands that suffering outlasts the spectacular, that after war there is the war-torn, and writes not only to document the loud, acute traumas of the powerless but also to chronicle the static and myriad traumas of everyday living under, and against, the powerful.

In this regard, Holnes is in deep conversation with Martinican political philosopher Frantz Fanon, who reminds us, in *The Wretched of the Earth*, that "in capitalist societies the educational system . . . the structure of moral reflexes handed down from father to son . . . the affection which springs from harmonious relations and good behavior—all these aesthetic expressions of respect for the established order serve to create around the exploited person an atmosphere of submission and of inhibition which lightens the task of policing considerably." In other words, culture is also war. And so, when a grandmother passes on a family recipe, as in the poem "Bread Pudding Grandmamma," and through that recipe a history, and through that history an understanding of just what it takes to endure, she is resisting. She is waging, as best she can, her own war against erasure and those who would have us erased.

This resistance as culture, as making, is a constant theme in *Stepmotherland*. Take, for instance, the poem "Poder," which, as the speaker tells us, is the Spanish word for "power" and

> is the same as the word for *I can*.
> *Poder*, one simple word banging the drum rhythm
> made by children's soles thumping against the earth . . .
>
> . . . where we find the power to turn suicide
> into sacrifice, the power to turn beasts
> into man, and man into martyr or miracle.

Or take, as another example, the poem "Praise Song for My Mutilated World," which ends on a note of such triumph that it becomes not just praise song but war cry:

> Pito and I save the negras in our arms from
> piedreros, drug dealers, and the cartel with
> our moreno swing-hips, dips, and spins to the two-beat
> carimbó drum rhythm stronger than the pulse
> thumping through my little boy body
> until I can't tell the difference
> between my corazón and the radio's ton-ton,

until our dream girls become our real women,
until we've praise-danced our world
back to being one that
little brown-black boys like me
can believe in.

To dance the world into something we can believe in is an admirable enough task, but if handled wrong, it can devolve into schmaltz or half-baked pamphleteering. Holnes avoids such a fate, first by tending to craft (notice in the passage excerpted above how well balanced and muscular his lines, how his use of consonance and assonance, the interplay of Spanish and English, give the poem its percussive rhythms, its propulsive energy, how he earns those last few lines) and second by eschewing ready-made binaries between good and evil, moral and immoral. Holnes's disdain for moral absolutes reveals itself as we move through the collection, away from the blatantly political poems toward poems of the body. Here, we are invited to explore questions of conquest and surrender in such a way that casts new light on everything read beforehand. The body becomes a site where violence and permission are negotiated. And somehow war, somehow politics, are rendered, in Holnes's able hands, erotic. Even if no less problematic, or messy.

It is this messiness that gives *Stepmotherland* its unique charm. It is a messiness born of honesty and vulnerability. Holnes's speaker never pretends to have all the answers. He is searching, interrogating, trying to make sense of this life just like the rest of us. In *Stepmotherland*, war, family, sex, politics, love, culture, language, all come together to create a world as compelling as it is wondrous. As a reader, I cannot ask for much more. Darrel Alejandro Holnes has given us a new anthem, a true praise song for our mutilated world.

—John Murillo,
Judge

Day, me say day-o. Daylight come and me wan' go home.

—Harry Belafonte

O, let my land be a land where Liberty
Is crowned with no false patriotic wreath,
But opportunity is real, and life is free,
Equality is in the air we breathe.

—Langston Hughes

FOREIGNER

When My Mother Gives Up Her American Dream to Marry My Father

She says it was *for love,*
as if the sound of the word
blowing in the wind

lifts the sails of her white dress
and sails her body back to my father
on his ship in the Panama Canal.

She says it was *for love,*
as if love were a place
above the clouds from which

she could see the earthrise
blanketed in dark space.
A sign, she says, told her for certain that

their lives would be wasted
if they were spent apart,
as if to say *for certain* were to

fold ginger lilies into the
Book of Corinthians on
the page with her favorite verse;

saving the flora to offer it
to a god she hadn't yet met, one day
when she'd believe in love again.

She always knew
it was coming, the harpy on
horseback, deity of her dreams with a

gray and white-feathered halo for a crown.
I never understood religious offering,
giving back to creators something

they could so easily take themselves, whether it be
taking her lamming for slaughter or taking her
dreams deferred of becoming a

nurse like Diahann Carroll's *Julia* on
U.S. TV stations that my mother watched
as a little Black girl in the Panamá of the 1960s.

Julia's good looks are an act of
defiance. Black women on
TV were never supposed to be beautiful.

My mother takes note and
offers my father her
velvet on their wedding night.

He crushes it to bring the
beauty out of the thing
like all men taught

by their fathers to
press a grape for wine or a
body for blood when it was the only

red the village men said he should take for a
wife, when she was the best kind of
woman the village men said he should take for

love. There's always a bit of
violence to sacrifice; flesh
crushed under the pressure of

other people's expectations, giving
life to the machos, the patrones, the pelaos, like me.
The blow of birthing machismo is only softened by

promises of sainthood, promises of
power over man now that her only
son was going to be one.

Today, she weeps when I don't go to church and
Hail Mary, and longs to return to the sea and a time when
the wind blew her dress perhaps in the

wrong direction. Tough for a mermaid to swim
upstream, tough for love to be like water, able to
sustain you any way the wind blows.

These days, she dreams of life at the
bottom of the sea. These days
breathing air feels like drowning.

Praise Song for My Mutilated World

Ode to the Japanese radio oozing hot tunes in
the hot afternoon of my childhood at age four in
La Ciudad de Panamá at my abuelo's house.
Ode to the Black women made of air and imagination who
Pito and I dance with in his living room in
La Rosita, the rosy part of Río Abajo
known for turning bullets into blooms.
Ode to Loalwa Braz, the early 90s Brazilian siren in Kaoma,
who seduces us into dancing with our dream girls
and away from the bullet-bitten bodies
plastered across the front page of La Crítica news.
Ode to the famous mulatto melody howling
from the bellows of the accordion on the record
and to the Portuguese words I pronounce in near-Spanish
as I try to sing along to the forbidden dance song:
A recordação vai estar com ele aonde for.
A recordação vai estar pra sempre aonde for.
There isn't much forbidden in my family
except piedra and hierba and the tiroteo from their trade.
There isn't much forbidden in my family
except pistolas y secuestros and chanchudos y
corruptos who've become piedra's slaves.
Pito and I save the negras in our arms from
piedreros, drug dealers, and the cartel with
our moreno swing-hips, dips, and spins to the two-beat
carimbó drum rhythm stronger than the pulse
thumping through my little boy body
until I can't tell the difference
between my corazón and the radio's ton-ton,
until our dream girls become our real women,

until we've praise-danced our world
back to being one that
little brown-black boys like me
can believe in.

Scenes from Operation Just Cause

FADE IN.

CUT TO:

EXTERIOR: U.S. INVASION OF PANAMÁ 1989

(Bird's Eye Shot)

They call this the tiny war,
la guerra tin-tin chiquitita,
but the last time the land shook,
it was emerging from the water.
Trémulo, trémulo, moviendo la tierra.
A strip of earth separating
a golden glaze from
the ocean's cerulean surface shakes.
El mar, la mar, brillantez marina.
The sun mirrors the
fish-like flesh of the sea.
Two continents join, and
the world of oceans divides.
El mar unido jamás será vencido.
And now the land trembles off
calamity's bottom lip,
emerging from a man's mouth,
de pie o muertos, pero nunca de rodillas!
El General speaks the country's true name:
tierra de peces, regrese a mi.
He shoots at the gringos with one last wish:
to win the war around the world's big ditch.

CUT TO:

INTERIOR – Home – NIGHT – 1989

My family is crouched on the floor in the master bedroom. The house shakes. Mama looks at my father.

PAPA
What?

Mama looks at us, her children, and then looks back at her man.

MAMA
God wanted them to be American.

The lamp smashes on the floor and a broken piece misses my eye and slices my left cheek. I see my own blood for the very first time.

BOY
Are the good guys here to get the bad guys, mommy?

MAMA
Let's hope.

The land tilts; it had seen more peace underwater where man does not breathe or bomb. My father spreads his arms over all of us on the floor; a mattress covers him.

FADE OUT.

20 de Diciembre, 1989: When the U.S. Invades Panamá

We pull GIs who've jumped from planes out of the Bay
and dress them in warm clothes, as if
doing so would make enough magic in this story to
save lives. The orange colors of our
mola cloths wrapped around their cold flesh
bring back a blush of red to the soldiers' bodies.
Our desperate knocks on their chests echo
a pulse back into their chambers. Then,
a rush of blood shoots into their hands
as they pull triggers to
save our father from Noriega's firing squad
for being too friendly with Uncle Sam.
Everyone needs a bit of saving,
a little money under the mattress, because
revolutions always happen on rainy days.
But they also end with a dance party, where we
paint happy faces over war wounds,
where spins around the ballroom
shake off the men the Invasion made us be.
There are a thousand and one nights of
twirling until the next bomb falls.
Magic is the distance time makes
between each full turn in a long tulle dress,
between the first and last beat, when, with a
boom, the dance song finally comes to an end.

When the Narcos Kidnap JuanFe

1

You stop driving
your car to school
like JuanFe did.
The school bus has bulletproof windows.
And witnesses.
You go by your mother's maiden name
so no one hears your father's
bling bling when they call for you aloud.
Somehow, this makes you look
more like her
when you cry.
Somehow, a river rises
when you weep
it floods your neighborhood.
You become good
at keeping secrets.
No one knows
about this river.
When the guardia asks for your address
you send him to the estuary,
where, in the tides,
you found the blanquita who loves
your mystery.
You learn to make love with shadows
watching.
She loves it like that,
all that Black.

2

You keep your nose clean
even when you could use
a little bump because there are
enough of those already
in the road for morenos
con plata like you,
brown men in the black:
enough money to be visible to thieves,
enough black to be victims of the police.
And you already struggle to drive
within the lines.
So you think:
better to sequester
yourself to the U.S.
than surrender to the narcos'
secuestro express,
their kidnappings at gunpoint
at any stoplight
between San Miguelito and Ancón
for whatever money can be
withdrawn from an ATM.
When the visa comes you sell
your mirror's many faces
for a single look for the passport pic.
One discarded face is JuanFe's
staring back at you
from behind
a bright light.
Another is of a deer
standing in the way
of a school bus,
too scared to move.

Another is of a driver
heading north
despite whatever
stands in his way.
Driver honks.
Driver accelerates.
Driver fails to
pump the brakes
hoping all roads,
regardless the slaughter,
will, at least, still
destinate.

The Art of Diplomacy

The diplomat kids at the international school were all from
somewhere else, and those of us who weren't, needed to be

so I pulled a Sean John shirt over my head as if
the logo were an American flag, although not the same one

President Bush saluted since nobody at school supported
American wars or military operations like the one that destroyed

El Chorrillo, the bombed ghetto behind my house where
I could still hear ghosts at night crying

socorro! as if even in death they never escaped
the flames. At school I wore a bandana like Tupac Shakur

and other rappers whom our raperos and reggaetoneros
imitated in their music videos.

There was always something more credible about
our moreno stories when they were

told to the beat of an African drum
played with an American gun

as if doing so made us Black cowboys or
the next closest thing: West Coast gangster rap gods

who rich kids worldwide, like the ones at my school,
pretend to be whenever they want "street cred."

To be a diplomat like our fathers is to serve
the public what they need to eat

like when Marcela speaks with little sympathy to me about her
moreno chauffeur's drug-addicted and jailhouse past

and I serve her Tupac lyrics: *First ship 'em dope and let 'em deal the brothers.*
Give 'em guns, step back, and watch 'em kill each other.

To be a diplomat like our mothers is to understand others whether or not
you're understood. *Not "black" like you*, Marcela says,

"black" as in poor. They fill their lives with drugs because
they can't afford much else, she attempts sympathy

while speaking to a teenage me rocking Timberland boots and
the most expensive urban wear my parents' money could buy.

Perhaps there was a star-shaped black hole
the size of the Canal in the Tommy Hilfiger flag

draped over my chest as if
my body were a casket.

Bread Pudding Grandmamma

We crack open the coconut and
    mix the fluids of el coco with cow's milk
like I mixed words with grunts and moos when
    speaking with my childhood fable friends.

My grandmother teaches me her recipe for bread pudding when
    I come home heartbroken from high school.
Together, we bake everyday pains into guilty pleasures.
    We mix torn apart bread-loaf backs into the batter—

always mixed in a ceramic bowl—
    and watch them move like tectonic plates.
I turn the earth at force with my spoon like
    turning through stages of teenage rebellion where
nothing stands firm beneath my feet and
    my mind, like bread, is an uneven sponge.

I add in brown sugar, *to taste*, she says,
    and eat some as we bake to feel
better about being called a *brownie* today in class—
    a little glucose for her day of tasting tears that
run down her cheeks as old age
    runs with my grandfather's mind.

We add white sugar, then vanilla, no almond extract,
    unless her monthly check has come in time.
If it hasn't, our palette will taste a richer sweetness—
    the soulful truth of Caribbean cuisine:
almond absence brings the vanilla out more.

Our hands mush together our pains with
a few grains of salt, *for style*, she says, with
    a few slices of butter, *the secret to life*
in each mixing bowl.

I'm the darling grandchild,
    her favorite, I believe.
At school there is trouble
    and medication for her is expensive,
so we make bread, bake bread,
    the sweet kind to satisfy our appetite.

She digs from the bottom of a jar for
    fruits soaked in wine—
Only the best ones.
    We add this last.

This is what gives it that taste man,
    any liquor is all right.

She talks, I smile.
    Eighty-six-years-old,
I believe her old hands and weak eyes
    but strong legs and big smile.

We empty it into the pan,
    bake it, and trade our worries for the aroma.
We breathe in the perfume of
    hard work on a hot afternoon,
forget that children can be mean,
    and that with wisdom comes age,
but with age comes ailment.

    Bake for one and a half hours,
and devour.

Poder

The difference between poetry and rhetoric
is being ready to kill
yourself
instead of your children
wrote Audre Lorde.
I say this now to the mothers who sent
their children north,
risking their babies' lives for
a better living
than chasing paper or running
from drug dealers
on the streets. The difference
between art and design means
being ready to die
for what you desire
others to achieve
through your work,
hours of your life gone forever
making a little, shiny, fragile thing.
I write to the mothers who send
their children north
never knowing if they'll make it
but hoping that even if they don't
their creations might mean more than just
the flesh and bone with which they're made
because they moved, because they desired.
So many are quick to dismiss
desire as too general a word
or this language as too simple
to power the constant thrust

towards betterment we call *life*,
but poetry is sometimes made of such things,
words used so often we take them for granted
and forget their power is in how they unite
existence through a common tongue.
In Spanish, the word for *power*
is the same as the word for *I can.*
Poder, one simple word banging the drum rhythm
made by children's soles thumping against the earth:
Po-der, po-der, po-der; the power of doing
in each disyllabic step of metric feet
moving us farther and farther
away from the word being just rhetoric,
into the structure of its design
where we find the power to turn suicide
into sacrifice, the power to turn beasts
into man, and man into martyr or miracle.
This is what makes miracles: a desire path
stretching seventeen hundred miles
through an armed border wall,
through electric barbed-wire fences—
A surge surmounting
all odds to rise beyond the stratosphere;
knowing this too is poetry.

for The Surge: Central American refugees marching to the USA

INMIGRANTE

Tú

In the music video it looks like Shakira is dying.

I want to die for you
       although we've just met,

give you my bones to help you stand taller
and my feet for you to walk on when yours are worn.

       This is what she sings, love
worth dying for.

Seven years ago, I loved her video

and now hear its song wailing in my head
as I struggle to hear what you're saying,

a good omen at Café Adobe,
       the setting of our first date.

Make love to me on this table for two.
I don't need my flesh if I have you.

So, devour my body as you need,
       breaking into the garden,

past the wall that keeps our home countries, my Panamá,
your Rwanda, out on the other side.

Your sins, washed in my old
blood and complexion, sing out.

Listen to the unusual
yodel in my throat,

a ballad as I nail my limbs to
this restaurant table:

*Eres tu amor, mis ganas de reír, el adiós que no sabré decir, porque nunca podré
vivir sin ti.*

But for this feast to nourish your body we must first pray
or at least say we believe in something.

I don't believe in this nation

but can in your naked grace. Come
make me a man   of faith.

Leave your body, too, if you'd like.

In my country I dreamed of leaving
my body all the time.

The scar below my right eye is
flesh broken by soldiers

trying to scare my mother
into telling them my father's whereabouts;

my sun-kissed undertone torn open reveals
an ancestor's sinless shame,

mejorando la raza.
But I don't want to be whiter, just free,

sweetly delivered into your dark matter,
and its boundlessness;

reborn into love, risen
in translation.

Conception

They say god made Texas   its own country;

a separate body of tangles and handles, of loon ducks and tumbleweed so

I brought us here to find salvation   but shouldn't have believed

undocumented miracles,   enough ground to break   but not enough for

a foundation   so let's construct a home

somewhere underneath the flesh   is an empty world

no longer a place for   ghosts, but for worshipping   each other.

Let my fingers push apart   your breasts and mark an address between them.

Your lips   reach into   my heart   and play house   with its

chambers,   a picture put up   with each kiss,

a photo of your father in every room   on fire   in iron skillets,

ashes spilt on the carpet   of the atrium,   a phoenix

or a vulture   atop the stove,   risen   or ready   to feast.

My hands reach   under your dress   and find

Mary   before she bore   the word   *immaculate*   onto our tongues.

I'm old-fashioned, so you pull off   robes   and give   yourself to me

to be   our own messiah,   merge our temples   and   write new

commandments   on these sheets   of smoke,   making love   to fire.

But this new religion is not witchcraft   we are just becoming holy   parents to

a second   city upon a hill   as the old one, too greedy,   quickly burns to char.

Wait.   Touch it.   Can you feel   our new city   kicking within you?

Can you see its   gated communities   press against your belly?   (Wink.)

Mansions   for us all inside.

How to Dream About a Woman

How to dream about a woman's grief filled lungs screaming *socorro!*
Sending you scrambling for the raft and life vest to survive the storm brewing
    inside her—

River rising fifteen shades of black & blue beating you
for not being buoyant enough to alone keep you three afloat.

How to dream about a woman's sharply turned lips saying you shouldn't have
tried to build an ark to save her, loved her or the child so soon,

terrified life's darkness would again be able to drown.

How to dream about a woman's calloused hands gaspingly reaching for air
as she is smothered by your mourning what you only briefly both had

by remembering, as she desperately closes her eyes
like fists and fights you to forget—

A woman you can't stop loving, come bruise or blood shine.
Hold her, if you must, and leap into the river, its consoling water breaking

your fall. This is how love dies quietly in its sleep,
sinking into currents of contusions and reverie.

ba•by

\ \ *n.* **1.** Auburn, gold, and blossom cherry: our fingers, two rings and my tongue along your ear/ Electric lighter, gas stove good time/ Praying for lightning. **2.** Man-made, made man, fire. **3.** This woman's need for the family lost to the guerilleros/ This man's efforts to be her village/ Inferno. **4.** A bump barring in the words *I don't love you anymore* as he kisses her belly for the Christmas card photo. **5.** The end of an argument in the emergency room. **6.** What we lost in the flames. \ \ *v.* **1.** To nurse, cure with promises, a cocktail of words, each word mixed in to strengthen the other/ *Marry me anyway.* **2.** To link by umbilical cord/ To cut the cord and hit the thing's bottom so we hear it breathe. **3.** To hear silence instead.

Pietà by Michelangelo: Marble, 1499

Even the Son of God's body must go cold when it dies
shivering, chicken skinned, and chilled to its core of cuero en cuero
save for a rough, frayed, modesty cloth he wears
as his flesh lay fading across his
Earthly mother's lap of robes that hang as
haggard and agonious as hangs her folded face of grief.
Her mourning and his mortality are forever
immortalized in Michelangelo's marble statue.
If it were painted, perhaps the many reds of man's red blood would
run on the river of Mary's robe's many blue hues; perhaps
the statue's grief would be brought to life by a mix of
cerulean and indigo swirling in crimson and scarlet.
But there is no scarlet for the woman who watches the
breath she gave her godly child float away from his body in a
last exhale. There is no scarlet for the man who
knew the world would betray him and still let it take his life.
There is no scarlet for the world who kills its young or for
the god who lets his son die. There is little color to this icon,
little paint to its face, only austerity's shadows, only divine's light
in the gray, in the marble, in the sorrow, in the white.

OTM or Other Than Mexican

Other than *que pedo*
We *que xopa*

Other than *ta bueno*
We *offi*

Other than *cosa*
We *vaina*

Other than *vato*
We *pelao*

Other than *amiguin*
We *fren*

Other than *coyote*
We ride *La Bestia*

Other than *¿Mande?*
We *¿Que cosa?*

Other than *no mames*
We *chucha*

Other than *culero*
We *hijueputa*

Other than *calmate guey*
We *tranquilo pana*

Other than *me vales madre*
We *me vales verga*

Other than *peda*
We *party*

Other than *chela*
We *pinta*

Other than *crudo*
We *focop*

Other than *el arte de engañar*
We *juega vivo*

Other than *pinta*
We *sopre*

Other than *llevarse el demonio*
We *cabrea*

Other than *huir*
We *chifear*

Other than *chava*
She *gial*

Other than *bonita*
She *pritti*

Other than *firme hina*
She *pai*

Other than *casita*
We *chanti*

Other than *pachanga*
We *rumba*

Other than *panzana*
We *preñada*

Other than *padre*
We *viejo*

Other than *nene*
We *chichi*

Other than *niños*
They *children*

Other than *fresh off the boat*
They *gringos*

Other than *hablar*
They *speak*

Other than *vivir*
They *be*

Other than *nosotros*
They *me*

Mirror Woman

1

She's made of mirrors,
        the breaking kind
that chase you to this America.

2

        You see the back roads of Smiley, Texas,
every time you see a naked woman,
                her bosom is an apple pie,
        a country neither of you knew existed.

3

                        But it's hard to swing for a white-picket dream
        when you see your reflection
                inside every womb
ready to be made a homerun.

4

A scorned mirror shatters
        its own flesh and shoots
                through you from every angle;
                        shards everywhere your blood used to be.

5

Look yourself in the eye.
Is that a ghost staring right back?
But how, when only your own flesh and blood
could look at you like that?

Marvelous Sugar Baby

A Black woman sings *azúcar!*
over polyrhythmic African drums
on the Latino radio stations
blazing from my smart phone
on the above-ground subway line
in Houston. *La negra tiene*
tumbao, sings queen Celia Cruz bluntly
about a señorita who doesn't sweat
the small stuff and is therefore
unstoppable
as she commands us all to dance
to the ton-ton of a conga drum.
But sugar is so soluble and
precious that all it takes is a drizzle
to end the night early
and send the band home.
You'd think stronger stuff
would come from sugarcanes
so hard to chop down that white men
once thought only the Negros
could do it. Perhaps
that's the thing about making,
the strongest structure is that which
is inevitably torn down.
This is where we find joy: a rumba despite
the high chances of rain at the Taco Milagro salsa night,
a sing-along about the sweetness of life despite
salty sweat drowning our faces
as the drum rhythm picks up

and our bodies move faster together
toward their own inevitable ends apart—

After Kara Walker

CITIZEN

Cristo Negro de Portobelo

It's when they see me naked that they finally believe
I'm from Panamá. The crucifix
hanging on my Black chest, underneath
the little hair I inherited from my father,
sweats as I perform what priests
and their laws call *unnatural acts*.
Only men grow body hair.
Only men are this dark and when
my hands finally darkened enough
to color even the blackest swans
I was sad to see them suddenly turn into wings,
plumed palms, hollow finger bones,
limp wrists. But then again, the struggle
of first flight against the moon's night
can be a freedom beyond heaven and
its wanting eternity. So now
rebellion is my new religion
or something else romantic and American
like a crownless king, perhaps an immigrant one
atop a throne, in native disguise.

Af•ri•can-A•mer•i•can•ize

\ \ *v.* **1.** To enchant by turning my meneo into a *bump & grind* against a hard bass-driven synth rhythm/ No longer a hand-hit on ton-tones, congas, and bongos/ No more rumba y azúcar, el sabor de los congos/ No more *tu pum-pum mami, mami no me van matar*/ Now I like that *boom boom pow, chickens jackin my style*/ Now *can I get a hey? Can I get a yo?/ You can get with this or* —wait— is that how it goes? **2.** To trade in Puma cleats for Air Jordans/ To refer to "futbol" as "soccer"/ As if it were a game between sock puppets. **3.** To root for a basketball team based on their colors even when you're from a suburb 3,000 miles south. **4.** To cross the border between real and pretense/ To really want them to win, to really want to fit in. **5.** To look at the people who look like you and see family. **6.** How I twist my bachata-dancing movidas when twirling my girl on the pista de baile/ Double-dutch jumps skipping ropes to escape lynch mobs or the long arm of the law coming after me for reaching into my pants for my phone or any other black, gun-like thing/ *Blackbirds, blackbirds, hanging from the wire. What do you do there? May we inquire?* **7.** To fly into the sky/ To become dark matter/ Letting the night blacken my brown/ To be more than a moreno from Panamá. **8.** Beyond the night, I'm becoming hypothetical/ Unable to be seen by the naked eye/ Beyond the night, I'm becoming a force forever expanding the universe.

African Klan Suit #2

African Klan Suit #2 by Michael Paul Britto: African Fabric
on Mannequin: 2010

The tribal pattern covering the
klansman's suit makes it
look like black sheep's clothing
designed to hide hatred
behind a Kente cloth.
Or perhaps smother it with
culture, the one thing the
Klansman can never burn on a
cross. Jesus didn't die for
style so there is no way to
bleach the robe back to white.
In this hood, the klansman
gives the K back to Kente.
In this hood, the klansman
gives the K back to Kunta.
In this hood, the klansman
gives the K back to King.
One way to enhance
an object is with
a fresh coat of paint.
What a riot when doing so
makes a work of art!
What a revolution when
such art paints history
where it's been erased

and can be worn
with a little elegance
to give us life,
a necessary
grace.

Ferguson, USA

When life gives you strange fruit
you make a sweet champagne
even though to make brut
you have to pay in spades.

You take the fruit's strange juice
and pour it in a cup.
Eat the pomace produce
like raisins in the sun.

Or let it hang there, ripe
and plump for crows to pluck.
Let juice ferment to wine.
Swill it around for luck.

Wrap it in paper bags.
Drop a few in an ice pail
and make your own price tags.
Sing out, *Nutcrackers for sale!*

And when that cop appears
offer him a cold cup,
before he sees your fear
and tries to lock you up

when white boys are chugging
and keg-standing this split,
when white girls are crying
to get another hit,
and even their parents
are addicted to it.

Do you have a permit to sell this strange fruit shit?

The cop asks you before
he takes a second swig.
This time, he sips and tastes
ambrosia in the brew
and sees that he could make
the same of me and you.

What will you do
when he shoots to
drain your strange juice?

Let the red bullet wound
fester like a sore?
Then, when your blood's on tap,
not to take it anymore?

In this darker-the-berry world,
in this Eden-before-the-fall,
a sweet tooth will lead everyone
to splash against a wall!

Links

Slaves. Sugar. Rum. Sweet. Liquor. Liquorices. Black. Brown. Cane. Back. Broken. Bent.

Over. Edge. Under. Water on deck. Links. Links. Shackled. Chains. Thunder. Storms.

Hard rain. Sleet. Snow. Shine. Sold by the pint. Links. Links. Journey cake.

Johnnycake. Baker's bread. Ginger root. Children. Good when dead. Links. Links.

Slaves. Sugar. Freedom. Daiquiri. Drink. Drunk. Marry. Me. Beaulah. I ain't no punk.

Ask. Claim. Force. Marry. Cheat. Divorce. Ring. Run. Mulatto. White cotton sun.

Sugar. Rum. And links. Links. Charming, charming, cherry. Charming, charming, Paul

Patch them up. Ship them then again trade them all. Links. Links.

Ode to My Father, The Captain

Praise be to my father. Glory be to his never-blinking
eyes, wide open in solidarity with the

unstoppable water flow between oceans and the endlessly swift
airstreams in the sky. Ever alert, armed only with his

compass and memorized maps of the stars,
he pilots the ship through locks in the Panama Canal to

turn tides on a dime in the dance of trade,
and unlock the Earth's many ancient water routes.

Honor be to my father for keeping us worldly with
rubber cargo from Indonesia for our sneaker soles,

and tantalizing tantalite cargo from Brazil for our iPhones
in a world where people are defined by their crazy love of foreign things.

Praise be to the captain's pepper-tongue
speaking orders in an island-infused English to the

ship's home squad while also speaking a smooth-sailing Spanish to his
canal crew of good-time-guy Pana-master pilots

for navigating the planet's sea of tongues with style and the graceful
tonetics of an articulate diplomat as any Black man

who is among the first captains of his kind would have to do.
Praise to the giants on whose shoulders my father stands, to the

shackled gallants packed top to bottom and shipped in galleons from
Badagry or Cape Coast Castle to West Indian plantations and then to our

isthmus to build and labor our canal. To the ancestors who guide my
father when his motors break with their celestial steering, with the

gentle push from their hands of sky, just as he guides me to steer my
Black-man body past us having once been considered cargo, past his now

commanding a foreign cargo ship, to me, one day, becoming the
wind sifting through all sails; to my, one day, becoming the

water through which all ships must navigate; to my, one day, becoming the
dark matter from which the stars hang at night, illuminating

the way home for all who have strayed or been stolen.
And now, kind captain, go home to rest. The last boost of

coffee has rained down from your thermos flask
and washed through your blood to mine. You who

cruise the moon around the world so tight, rest
sweetly as you sail home tonight.

Breaking & Entering

Sleep by Kehinde Wiley: Oil on Canvas: 2008

Only beasts are supposed to hibernate.
But this brother has been lying there
for years. Truth isn't a news headline.
Between the lines lay his body, between
brush strokes
his soul ascends doing those things
portraits rarely capture:
giving life, giving face, serving.
A Black man's body
on display hangs in a museum.
He appears wrapped in a bed sheet
covering his private parts as if
he was a sexless Christ.
But perhaps it's just respectful to cover
a dead man or to give him wings—
him wings
any better burial than the other brothers got,
those over there, just left on the street.

in memory of Javier Ambler

Angelitos Negros

In the Mexican film, "Angelitos Negros," both parents appear with skin as white as
      a Gitano's bolero sung by an indigena accompanied by the Moor's guitar
bleached   by celluloid in 1948   when in America
      the world's rainbow was polarized into   black & blanco.

In the film, Pedro Infante plays Jose Carlos   and sings
      Angelitos Negros, while sitting in a chapel,
      asking the painter of the church's art to paint a picture with Black angels
who look like his character's dark-skinned daughter,   a child his wife refuses to accept:

    ¿Pintor, si pintas con amor, porque desprecias su color
                     si sabes que en el cielo   *también los quiere Dios?*

    Tonight I sing the same song for my morenos absent from my cathedral walls:

O painter, painting with a foreign brush to the rumba of its old world bolero.
      Listen to our angel's chorus of inocentes morenos muertos.

We morenos in the barrio cook a gumbo quilombo, our little taste of heaven
      with matches and propane and coal stones under a pot of cabra y culebra.

We morenos are brown turned black,   burnt by fire fired from guardia guns
      shooting us congos   for the   chanchudos of a rabiblanco legislador.

Listen to los pelaos in the favelas kicking
      around the soccer ball   de pie a pie de pie a pie de pie a pie cabeza cabeza

                     gol!

forced out of their homes   by a world class stadium   they can never afford to get into,
                    forced into a life in the prison   of their streets.
They too deserve to be painted.

                    ¿Pintor, si pintas con amor, porque desprecias su color?

                    Now, Eartha Kitt sings Pintame Angelitos Negros,
          the same Andrés Eloy Blanco poem Infante   set to song
on thrift store vinyl   playing in homemade YouTube clips.
                    Through my headphones I hear Kitt raise her voice high enough
to swallow Evening   if it does not give her a sky
                                        with dark-skinned angels in its clouds tonight.

          Then dusk falls over the continent built on
     shadows, shackles, and shame as the news paints yet another Negro as the devil.

Broken-winged Blackbird, three shades of jade, fly into the dark matter of outer space.
          Perhaps up there is a better painter, better god for us all   to obey.

PATRIOT

The Down-Low Messiahs

In his hands I was a cup overflowing with thirst—
Finally, in New York City, eager to bless his
face during this heat wave, eager to be a fire hydrant
Holy Grail. Sweet deliverance, this was my death,
salivation from his sins, from his woman
(and the ways she too *must* love)
as I wish I had been from mine—
A bath of silky steam fogs up the mirror, *see no evil.*
Strong water pressure, hard rain, loud fall, *hear no evil.*
A small hotel room soap bar cleans off residue
left by his adhesive embrace of my lips
and washes my mouth out for *speaking evil,*
calling god's name out in vain again and again—
And here I am, punishing myself for shining
the *other* light, here I am learning how to tell a lie.
But it's too late—we've bitten too many fruits
and cannot relearn the old world.
Skins stretching and sweat quenching
fire-starting words—
The half-made mold of her on his arms
cracking slightly when we embrace.
The virgin on my medallion hits my chest
each time I kneel in front of him to
pray. My ring finger slides *forbidden*
down his thighs in communion with
flesh, its burn and concurrent healing.
Oh Lord, its reddening appetite—

Power Bottom

What can come from
　　　　perfumes of rotten fruit

every time you pull me
　　　　closer,　　　　push me harder,

scream my name. Tighter,
　　　　my reach pulls the rope.

Please, don't stop. Bodies
　　　　ring in harmony with

the rope's singing chord. I avoid
　　　　seeing ghosts by rolling my eyes

to the back of my head.
　　　　But even there I find them,

strange fruit, hanging from old oaks,
　　　　broken, bent, whipped, and bled.

So I reach to break the rope
　　　　Please stop. Don't—

When it's all too much to bear.
　　　　But instead my nails dig

into your back as I swivel and ride
　　　　pain, twisting into each lash.

There are too few of us to touch tonight
        and though I see trees in your eyes

ordering me to call you Master, rope pulled
        bruising my skin black,

you say *this is love. Tighter. Tighter!*
        Light a match, catch afire.

Smoke rises.

A trail of tiny ashes; the hanging
        scent of blood burnt leaves.

Vinyl

A scratched record from the thrift store serenades as
loneliness aways from our holy bones and hides
beneath the television set; its face has turned black.
Perhaps the TV set is off, and this turns us on. Perhaps
after the credits come the world's oldest form of
entertainment: a feathered set of cuffs, a pair of
heels, and me piercing your nipple with a golden spear.
A spotlight lights us from the flashlight on your cell phone.
Yes, perhaps we are stars on camera.
Perhaps its pornography in the 70s.
Perhaps a love scene. Perhaps
cigarette smoke on the silver screen was sexy then, is sexy now.
Is nostalgia the tartest apple in our mouths?
Whisper your favorite lines from the song into the
camera moving side to side around the room:
I don't know why . . . nobody told you . . . how to unfold . . . your love.
Romeo, burn me like the city in your name.
We are an empire in its final days. We are Icarus flying
too close to the sun. Phoenixes rise from
leather whips and unlinked chains.
Love is an addiction to poppers, PrEP, and shame
and temptation is tobacco ash
burning down the arch of your back when
a song we used to know by The Beatles
brings out the sweet blues in the pain.

I Always Promised I'd Never Do Drag

You liked me as *straight* as a man
in love with another could ever be,
and I did too. But you also loved
women, how their backs widen
where hips appear, how their necks
swerve like swans swallowing water
when they call your name,
their long hair stroking your face
as they wake from nestling
your chest the morning after.
So here I am wearing the wig I made
in the image of the blondes you preferred
but said you could never love, applying eyeliner
but not for it to run. *I will never
love him again*, I fearlessly announce to the mirror
as I beat my face with powder base into submission,
as if one could ever fall out of the hero's arms and
not back into peril. Tonight,
for the first time, I dance to save myself
from distress, becoming the one woman
you'll never have instead. Tonight, at the Esta Noche bar in
the Mission District, I'm distance. The closest I ever came
to doing drag before was when I was crowned prom king
but chose instead the queen's tiara;
cubic zirconia somehow closer
to real than the king's cardboard cut-out crown.
Tonight, I'm Diamante, extravaganza eleganza,
a gurl singing shine to the Yoncé record,
declaring myself the Queen B of the Night, singing
take all, of me, I just want to be the girl you like, the kind of girl you like

sashay-shante-strut-shimmy shining on stage,
dunking it like an Oreo, making the masses
shake they asses at the command of
the scepter firmly in my hand. A king,
I queen so hard my earth-quaking rule
breaks the laws of nature; flesh-colored spanx and
control-top leggings tuck it away
where the sun don't shine.
A black lace-up corset covers the missing rib
but lets the rest of me hang out enough to werk
and soak up applause from an audience
who loves this boy dressed as girl,
boy dressed as girly man, boy dressed as man
enough to drag, man dragging on,
man moving on, man gone.

Arroz Con Pollo

Arroz Con Pollo by Jean-Michel Basquiat:
Acrylic and Oil on Canvas: 1981

In the painting, a woman offers her breast for
the bird who enters stage right
on the man's tray. But it's not
sexist expressionism. The bird too
offers her its breast. I can't help
but feel sorry for the man,
caught in the middle, serving
both predators their prey.
Although, I suppose in the end
she will eat the bird. But does
such devouring really make her
the one in most control? A bird
offering its body clearly wants
to be consumed by another's
desire, so perhaps the bird is more
in control than the hungry woman.
But does a matter of appetite always have
to be reduced to power? The fork appears
between one breast and another. Is love
always about dividing the heart?
Although really, love may
have nothing to do with
the scene in this painting,
it's so rarely ever present
where flesh is offered
in exchange. If it were about love

there'd be no hunger
or need for a tray.
If it were about love
we'd all come
to the table
satisfied.

Joseph on Knowledge in the Biblical Sense

The first time since the pregnancy,
first time we tried touch,
it just didn't feel right.
Mary isn't really mine, you know.
So immaculate, belonging alone
to *clean*. There isn't much pure about me.
Nor did I ever want to be a motherfucker,
the angel promised more.
I need her to be more than a holy
lace veil, a pendant, and grace. Perhaps soon
I will come to know her better,
bite the fruit she serves
as prey, teeth into rind, tongue into body,
milk of honeyed promise
running in snake-shaped streams down my neck,
before this was considered falling,
before feeding was a kind of disgrace.
The second time, she revealed the soft
underside of her wrists, a rushing pulse—
My fingers rising up her calves,
en route to her faith, made it quiver, made it sing.
Voices raised on high, an anointing—
Her oil smoothened Adam's roughness out of my skin,
her waters washed *original* from our sin.
By morning I had learned, our virginities
somehow still intact, why hers was
worthy of my worship.

All Legs Lead to Naomi Campbell

We wear "crowntis," gender-
bending crown/tiaras tilted to the side
like we LGB royalTy,
like we long legs on a catwalk, smoking
up the haus with our
hot sex-kitten heels
with our stomp and strut
until the windows are foggy
and the bloggers are out
of breath and edges,
until we've snatched
and slayed the runway at Fashion Week
wearing everything
China is selling online
that Americans haven't
yet Columbused.

When I cross the streets
of Kreuzberg, and you
the streets of Hong Kong,
there are no breadcrumb trails.
These big city streets
are wider than any runway
but still we toe in style
to the Späti for beer
or to the rooftop for
cockatoos and secret teas
with grandmother-in-laws
and ghosts who only speak Cantonese.
But still we stiletto
or loafer or boat shoe

while running upstairs,
while hanging from ladders,
while climbing from the rooftop
to the skies.

There are such few of us
left standing these days after
the nightclub shooting at Pulse in Orlando,
after the lobotomies or
electroshock therapy,
after AIDS,
after passing for straight,
after passing for white and white and white—

Naomi Campbell
is a sunset over
the 7 train on our way
to get dumplings with
your new partner
while reading poems
about your ex or horses in Iceland,
both who took you for a ride.
Naomi Campbell is
a dark shadow in a dream
your cousins don't realize
will save your uncle. Naomi Campbell
is a fire hydrant you unleash after
Romeo burnt my city down.

In another era, we are
locked up loonies.
In another era, we are
deities. Tonight, we are
throwing Blackberry phones,
dark-juiced and dangerous,
at whomever dares
stand in our way
or tell us how or who to love.

Strut your stuff with me, Black Diamond.
Come on, let's swallow the sun
and burn bright into the night
until our bellies are filled with
so much hubris
no man can ever put our kinship or kind asunder.
Filled with so much hubris,
we put god herself to shame.

for Rosebud

Rihanna & Child

The rude girl is with child in the Instagram pic. It's not her baby.
She wears a costume that conservatives may describe as *exotic* and *revealing*.
I call her *mi pana* and *mi pai*. The baby pulls sequins off her bustier.
But she's not afraid she won't shine. I was raised by her kind.

She shows us how to celebrate carnival as a #badgirl
goddess, tantalizingly #wifey material, playing
a benevolent stepmother with #milf appeal, taking
a break from dancing to hush a child in her auntie's laundry room.

Over half a million followers *like* this portrait of Rihanna
as the Black Madonna. In it her voluminous hair is a halo, her shiny
headdress is a crown, a beaded curtain frames her
as a domestic deity with a washing machine for a throne.

Her breast sits ready to be clutched for comfort by
the bawling majesty in her arms. Over half a million
followers hail woman for nestling babe against her
bejeweled bustier. Millions more were raised by her kind.

Millions more once nestled on the chest of a mother's uniform
or on the costume of an auntie close enough to be a stepmom
taking care of others on break from dancing
soca or murga in the parade.

I was raised by her kind, dazzling and Amazonian,
running so fast through the hairspray that her wig almost
bursts into flames. She who fills beach dunes with matches,
feathers, rhythms, and milk bottles.

Her nude arms waving at parade people walking by,
her ribs cracking where the DJ drops the beat.
She is not afraid to die. Yes, I was raised by
women like that. I was raised by her kind.

Naturalization

I haven't yet come out to my fam

    and I'm dating a white man named Matt.

Everyone has a part of themselves they keep private,

    these days the secret is their issues with race

    or desire.   Mamá always wanted

to be American, but she'd read in Essence Magazine

    about how its Black women

    were the least married in the country

    because ball players preferred white women on their arms.

Can you hear her crying

    as I play   ball   with my white boyfriend?

Hand jobs are the latest

    sex act in fashion. But then again,

    love is   an older kind of allegiance   than citizenship.

Sometimes,

I wear a cop uniform

during sex and throw my lover

behind bars. This role play is not called

Black Lives Matter. It's called

Love and Basketball. Matt plays

the white college ball player

I've arrested for slipping   a roofie into   my drink

while I was undercover at a frat party.

And now, in jail,   he begs for my   forgiveness.

I tell him no one man can save him

from a system; mass incarceration

is the American way. But I, at least, can apply

some lube and help   ease the pain.

Don't believe this part;

it's too dark to be true.

The American Dream

is not a fantasy. It's as real as   the resurrection

of turkey on Thanksgiving   and the healing properties of   apple pie.

There isn't much difference these days

between religion and history; if you believe it so

then that's how it happened. People believe more

in their points of view than in facts. Maybe I shouldn't

be any different. Maybe I'll just believe

my mother already knows her son

is in love with   American Jesus or some other

white man.   Mmm. . . Yes,

I believe we all know it,   to some degree,   a truth   so universal

others, on some level, *must*   know it too,

if only they could   make belief.   Then maybe,

just maybe,   the rest could finally

be as free or   American   as I've just now   come to be.

Black Parade

Coming out isn't the same as coming to America

except for the welcome parade

put on by ghosts like your granduncle Hector

who came to New York from Panamá in the 50s

and was never heard of again

and by the beautiful gays who died of AIDS in the 80s

whose cases your mother studied

in nursing school. She sent you to the U.S. to become

an "American" and you worry

she'll blame this country

for making you a "marica,"

a "Mary," like it might have made your uncle Hector.

The words "America" and "marica" are so similar!

Exchange a few vowels

and turn anyone born in this country

queer. I used to watch *Queer as Folk* as a kid

and dream of sashaying away

the names bullies called me in high school

for being Black but not black enough, or the kind of black they saw on TV:

~~black-ish, negro claro, cucco.~~

It was a predominately white school,

the kind of white the Spanish brought to this continent

when they cozened my ancestors from Africa.

There was no welcome parade for my ancestors back then

so, they made their own procession, called it "carnaval,"

and fully loaded the streets with egungun costumes,

holy batá drum rhythms, shouting and screaming in tongues,

and booty dancing in the spirit.

I don't want to disappear in New York City,

lost in a drag of straightness.

So instead, I proceed

to introduce my mother to my first boyfriend

after I've moved her to Texas

and helped make her a citizen.

Living is trafficking through ghosts in a constant march

toward a better life, welcoming the next in line.

Thriving is wining the perreo to soca on the

Noah's Arc pride parade float, like you're

the femme bottom in an early aughts gay TV show.

Surviving is (cross-)dressing as an American marica,

until you're a 'merica or a 'murica

and your ancestors see

you're the king-queen of Mardi Gras,

purple scepter, crown, and krewe.

Homecoming

Our mother always wanted me to go to an HBCU
but I never even applied–too afraid I wasn't Black enough.

Tupac-quoting, hip-hop standoffs, Tyler Perry marathon-watching,
cafeteria-grits-loving crews debating whether to add hot sauce or sugar or cheese—

It was all Greek to me; culture written in the tongue of
someone else's empire.

But then my boss, Ms. Daisy, called me "King Kong."
And it was just another gunshot echoed,

bleeding through the clouds, soaking the sky in
unscalable sound. I let it bleed

until the birds fell from the sky, until we believed god
had sent yet another plague. But then Jerome taught me

"Baby Love" by the Supremes, and the ways Diana
and her girls dared to Detroit the radio

and signify to the Black stations they were "colored"
and to the white stations that they were "safe."

But then Carl taught me American Beauty red roses
and Hallmark Valentine Day greeting cards

and how it's the thought that counts when
the whole world is made of symbols.

And right then I saw that all along, all along,
I had mistaken my spade for a big spoon,

and I, too, by the world and its pop culture, had been raced,
though not erased, somewhere between Beyoncé concert documentaries

and chitterlings I had graduated
Migration University

and finally become someone's "bae,"
someone's "homie," someone's N-word,

someone's son.

Notes . . .

Praise Song for My Mutilated World (page 5)
 References Adam Zagajewski, "Try to Praise a Mutilated World"
 References "Lambada" by Kaoma

Scenes from Operation Just Cause (page 7)
 "Operation Just Cause" was the code name for the U.S. invasion of
  Panamá, an operation allegedly designed for the arrest of the dictator
  of Panamá, General Manuel Noriega, a former CIA intelligence
  source
 Written after screenplay poems by A. Van Jordan in *M-A-C-N-O-L-I-A*

Poder (page 17)
 "The difference between poetry and rhetoric / is being ready to kill /
  yourself / instead of your children" –Audre Lorde, "Power"

Tú (page 20)
 References Shakira, "Tú"

ba•by (page 25)
 Written after definition poems by A. Van Jordan in *M-A-C-N-O-L-I-A*

OTM or Other Than Mexican (page 27)
 Incorporates a mix of mostly Mexican or Chicano slang and colloquial
  terms with Panamanian slang and colloquial terms

Marvelous Sugar Baby (page 32)
 References *A Subtlety, or the Marvelous Sugar Baby* by Kara Walker: Sculp-
  ture in Sugar: 2014
 References Celia Cruz, "La Negra Tiene Tumbao"

Cristo Negro de Portobelo (page 36)
 The Black Christ is a celebrated Catholic icon (sculpture) in the town of
  Portobelo, Panamá, since 1658
 Dedicated to Oscar Gutiérrez-Fernández

Af•ri•can-A•mer•i•can•ize (page 37)
References El General, "Tu Pum Pum"
References Black Sheep, "The Choice is Yours"
References Black Eyed Peas, "Boom Boom Pow"
References "Blackbird," an African American double-dutch song
Written after poems by A. Van Jordan in *M-A-C-N-O-L-I-A*

Ferguson, USA (page 40)
References Langston Hughes, "Harlem"
Echoes Harryette Mullen

Angelitos Negros (page 53)
References the film by the same name, directed by Joselito Rodríguez, and
its title song, "Angelitos Negros" by Pedro Infante, which is based on
the poem "Píntame Angelitos Negros" by Andrés Eloy Blanco

The Down-Low Messiahs (page 56)
"In his hands I was a cup overflowing with thirst" –Eduardo C. Corral,
"Our Completion: Oil on Wood: Tino Rodríguez: 1999"

Vinyl (page 59)
References "Still My Guitar Gently Weeps" by The Beatles

I Always Promised I'd Never Do Drag (page 60)
References Beyoncé, "Partition"
Echoes Mark Doty, "Esta Noche"

Arroz Con Pollo (page 62)
Arroz con pollo (rice with chicken) is Panamá's national dish

All Legs Lead to Naomi Campbell (page 65)
Dedicated to Rosebud Ben-Oni

Rihanna & Child (page 68)
References Anne Sexton, "Her Kind"
Dedicated to my mother

Photograph by Beowulf Sheehan

DARREL ALEJANDRO HOLNES

Darrel Alejandro Holnes is an Afro-Panamanian American writer and is the recipient of a National Endowment for the Arts Literature Fellowship in Creative Writing (Poetry). His poems have previously appeared in the *American Poetry Review*, *Poetry*, *Callaloo*, *Best American Experimental Writing*, and elsewhere. Holnes is a Cave Canem and CantoMundo fellow who has earned scholarships to the Bread Loaf Writers' Conference, Fine Arts Work Center in Provincetown, Postgraduate Writers Conference at Vermont College of Fine Arts, and residencies nationwide, including a residency at MacDowell. His poem "Praise Song for My Mutilated World" won the C. P. Cavafy Poetry Prize from Poetry International. He is an assistant professor of English at Medgar Evers College, a senior college of the City University of New York (CUNY), where he teaches creative writing and playwriting, and a faculty member of the Gallatin School of Individualized Study at New York University.